I0152879

A simple formula to happiness and success

LIFE
TRANSFORMATION

"The Amazing Way"

"For the Open Minded ... the Disbelievers, Naysayers & the Curious"

Author: JP TI

LIFE TRANSFORMATION
Published by JP TI
Copyright © 2014 by JP TI

ISBN 978-0-9929781-0-5

First printing: 2014
London, United Kingdom.
www.inspiredbyjp.com

Ordering information:
Go to the website, to the regular online stores and to one of JP TI's event.

To be inspired and know more about upcoming events:

Follow JP TI on Facebook: JPtransformationalinspirer,
www.facebook.com/JPtransformationalinspirer

Watch clips now available on YouTube:
www.youtube.com/user/inspiredbyjpti

Follow on Twitter: @inspiredbyjp

Get in contact:
Email: jp@inspiredbyjp.com

DEDICATION

I dedicate this book to you! The concepts, lessons and tips included in this book will guide you and help you in you search to find happiness and success!

I dedicate this book to all of the people that are living a life that they think they do NOT control, to all of the people who feel that they are not happy, who feel like they are underachieving and as if they are not living to their full potential. I also dedicate this book to all of the successful people who think that they are not successful, even when everyone around them tells them they are.

☺ Happy → not full potential → unsuccessful in life
☹ Unhappy → Successful in "paper or CV" → unhappy in life

This book is dedicated to everyone in this universe, with all my love, good thoughts and positive energy, I will aim to show you some of the best and easiest ways to deal with any of the challenges we all face in life, in order to be the happiest you have ever been, as well as the most successful you will ever become.

CONTENTS

ACKNOWLEDGEMENT 9
PREFACE..11
INTRODUCTION 15
A LITTLE ABOUT JP TI..19
GRAPHICAL SUMMARY 21
CHAPTER 1 23
CHAPTER 2 25
 2.1 BUILDING BLOCKS..25
 2.2 FOUNDATIONS 33
CHAPTER 3 41
 3.1 SELF ASSESSMENT 41
 3.2 ASK YOURSELF SOME CRUCIAL QUESTIONS 45
 3.3 FINDING YOUR SKILLS AND STRENGTHS.....................48
CHAPTER 4 53
 4.1 TYPES OF ACTIONS 55
CHAPTER 5 59
 5.1 LIMITING BELIEVES 60
 5.2 HABITS...62
 5.3 THE CONCEPT OF TIME 63
CHAPTER 6 65
 6.1 THE MAIN LAWS 65
 6.2 EXTRAS – CONCEPTS & COMMON LIMITING
 BELIEVES..73
 6.3 THE CREATIVE PROCESS...81
CHAPTER 7 85
 7.1 HEALTH (& EXERCISE)...85
 7.2 PERSONAL FINANCES & FINANCIAL INTELIGENCE 93
FINAL RECAP 99
OTHER ACKNOWLEDGEMENTS..101

ACKNOWLEDGEMENT

I want to start by thanking all the people I have ever met and helped me become who I am, in particular all my friends and people who support me, including:

Steph, Isabella and Sofia
Elaine & Frank
Mum & Valen
My brothers, sister and their families
Doug
Pupi & Juanpi, and my Moo family
Kriss
Belynda
KK
Peter
Tom
Ximena
Rose
Sarah
Alex
Jonpaul
Esme
Hannah
Richard
Sam
Laura
CJ
Storm
David Lloyd Kings Hill's gang
Fitness First Liverpool St.'s team
All my friends
All the people that have supported me before and after I discovered the formula ☺

PREFACE

"Once upon a time, I used to believe anything was possible ... then I stopped believing in the impossible and started only believing in possible ... Now, I just ... BELIEVE!"

JP TI

There is one overall objective I am looking to achieve and that is to be able to help as many people as I can, including that person sitting next to you on the tube, on the train, at the pub, at the gym, at work, that person that may be struggling with the smallest nag or the biggest problem they think they have to face without knowing how.

I want and plan to reach people from every walk of life, every social status, level of wealth or education. These theories are universal and applicable to anyone, wherever they live or come from, whatever their background.

If you were to define me, I would like you to think of me as a "Transformational Inspirer". I want to be able to share what I have learnt, in order for you to learn and find your own purpose in life so that you feel inspired to transform your life.

Ultimately, this is not about me. This book is about you.

You have made the decision to open this book because you desire the guidelines and methods to happiness and success. Through sharing my own knowledge and experiences with you, you are about to learn a series of lessons. It is with these lessons that I hope to provide an insight into how you can apply this knowledge in reality and I want to help you in any way that I can.

It could take you years of suffering, misfortunes, misunderstandings, failures, heart breaks, as well as years of expensive psychotherapy, and you still may not be told, learn nor understand what I am about to share with you.

In my view, this is a combination of the reasons why people say we "like learning from our own experiences" and the need to a) go through such a painful experience that give you what the experts call "Leverage" enough to change, combined with b) several books on self help and the right "knowledgeable" people to open up to and learn from.

What I am sharing with you in this book are some of the most powerful, thought provoking, mind blowing laws and tools to transform yourself, your way of thinking and your life, but only if you are ready to see through it. The "formula" is quite simple, you already have all the ingredients and you can even mix them at your own pace, time, and steps. It is completely up to you.

I want to make sure it is clear that what I am about to tell you is already available to you in many ways, as there are many people sharing some of the information and laws all over the world upon which I based my principles and techniques. Most importantly, **you already have all of the knowledge within you**. All I am trying to do is to make you aware, to share some of my experiences and lessons and the key principles, rules, steps, and processes I have developed and followed. They may resonate with you or relate to some of your situations and experiences to some degree, so you can replicate them or use them as a benchmark. Hopefully you will then be able to use these, as a stepping-stone to achieve what you thought was impossible.

I hope this book helps you with the start of your journey, to finally learn and understand how **simple** life is and how **beautiful and amazing** you can make it and that your thirst for learning and understanding will continue to grow.

If you are already there, I hope you find something new or useful for yourself, your friends or relatives.

I welcome your feedback and comments and I hope to receive all of your good energy, as I am sending mine to you right now! **Even if we may not know each other personally... I love you! And this book is the way I found to show it to you.**

INTRODUCTION

This book should be read as a whole, taking into consideration each part, chapter, component, concept, term, picture. It is a holistic formula that if you consider, understand and apply, it will change you to the core and will help you produce all the results you can dream of ... and **achieve your own LIFE TRANSFORMATION!**

In more practical terms, I approached the task of creating this book as a guide, where I aim to bring together what I believe most books I have had the blessing to come across don't do. This is a combination of:

- **Sharing the Laws of the universe and practical application to "every day" life, in order to learn to master your thoughts, and more specifically your subconscious thoughts over your conscious ones; or what most of us have learnt to call emotional intelligence**
- **Sharing the understanding of the basic forces behind happiness and success, – what I call the "Building Blocks" – simplifying the way to provide this information, so that everyone can understand it, with simple concepts and practical tools provided to help internalise them.**

What is happiness? What is success? I have discussed this at length with people, read, studied and learnt as much as I could about it.

Yes! I finally cracked it! For almost 20 years I have been looking for the "formula", reading books about success, reading biographies of successful people, articles in the magazine and papers, even trolling down the rich lists to research about people in them. I obviously was geared towards material success, but nonetheless I was looking into and applying it to other fields as well.

People think that they can either be happy or successful and not both - you can be either and not realise. For example, you may think that finance is a reflection of success, or perhaps you are desperate to be a mum and you don't feel successful or happy unless you have reached that. But often you are not successful until you realise that you are, for example through being grateful.

In a really summarised way ... happiness and success are "relative" and "subjective" terms. Each one of us has our own definition. So what I have come up with is what I think could help you achieve your definition of happiness and success. Alternatively, you may not even be sure what both of those terms mean to you; it is my aim to help you to cement your definition and to create your own vision.

Before I go into the detail of the book, I would like to make a statement:

I want to do something different! I want to do something that most authors and other books don't. Instead of asking you to read the whole story for you to try to work out the meaning and true formula, I want to tell you straight away. Although I understand you need to work it out for yourself, and there is no one solution for everyone, I would like to attempt to summarise everything in one word.

The formula for happiness and success is ... HABITS! ☺

Of course it is much more complex than that, but that is because we complicate things in life. But life can be simple and easy. I have been lucky enough to encounter, learn and understand the key concepts we

need to master in order to modify our habits to achieve what we want, whatever that is.

But one thing I can promise you: if you change your habits and apply these consistently, you will be happier and you will succeed at whatever you set yourself to do.

A LITTLE ABOUT JP TI

If I am completely honest, I have to admit I never thought I would be doing this and reaching out to people in this way, not only for the self-doubt and belief that I was not "qualified" enough – which I also thought would be the criticism from the "experts" – but worse, because I would expose my fears and experiences to people and for this they would laugh at me, all leading to loss of privacy to start with and much worse after that. Sounds a bit judgemental, fearful, and scary, doesn't it? ☺ But yes, that was me before I wrote this beautiful book.

So why the change of heart you may wonder?

It is because I hit rock bottom and I needed to open myself to learning, to change, because some days I could not bear the pain anymore.

It is also because I came across very special, good people.

And it is thanks to some of these events and feelings that that I experienced, that I came across some of the basic theories and knowledge, which all resided in me, but that I needed to find within me.

And it is because of all of this, that I realised that I had to share it with others, in order to help others too.

Some people I have met over the years, and particularly as I wrote and share drafts of this book, mentioned I should share a bit about my background, as it may resonate and help you understand where I come from and my perspective in life.

- I am originally from Argentina, and I was born in a small city call Posadas.
- I am from a very mixed race background (Germany, Poland, Spain, Native Indians-Guarani ... who resided in Brasil, Paraguay and finally Argentina).
- I have travelled and moved around a few countries. I lived in Argentina, USA, Chile and the UK.
- I moved to the UK in order to continue my passion for restaurants and get into Merger&Acquisitons (M&A) at a major Investment Bank, which I managed to do.
- I have been an Entrepreneur since an early age.
- I got married to a beautiful lady and I have 2 beautiful Daughters.
- Currently working in Banking but also working on projects to contribute to society and help make a difference in this world and this life.
- I have a PhD on myself; I have been studying it for 30+ years ☺
- I have another PhD from the University of Hard Knocks ☺
- I have a Business and management Degree and a Post-Graduate in International Finance.
- I am also a qualified in Personal Training, Fitness & Nutrition
- I unfortunately divorced the beautiful lady I married, and it is mainly for this reason that I have come to learn what I learnt, thanks to the journey I started after such painful event
- I feel re-born, I am transformed, as I have had to re-asses my values and priorities, and re-define my life purpose, which I am working on day by day, by way of building and applying new habits.
- I feel, at last, like a Matured Man ... I feel, at last, happiness & success ... I feel free and ready to LOVE!
- At last, I BELIEVE!

20

GRAPHICAL SUMMARY

The following set of blocks and pillars can help represent in an image what I have tried to share with you in this book. Although I actually do not cover them in the exact order in the following chapters, it may help you focus on the overarching concepts. I hope you enjoy it. I do not expect you to agree with everything I put forward, but if you take at least one thing that helps you be happier, you are helping us both achieve part of this amazing goal! Thank you!

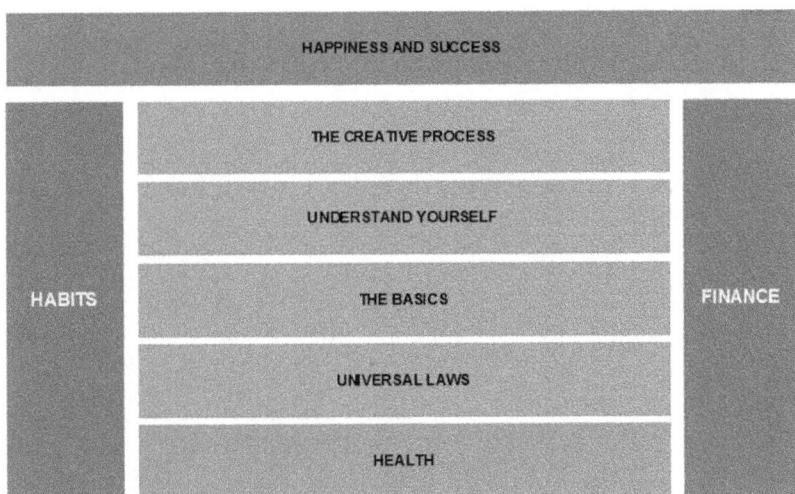

	HAPPINESS AND SUCCESS	
HABITS	THE CREATIVE PROCESS	FINANCE
	UNDERSTAND YOURSELF	
	THE BASICS	
	UNIVERSAL LAWS	
	HEALTH	

Remember ... *"LIFE IS A MARATHON ... NOT A RACE"*

CHAPTER 1
ASK YOURSELF SOME QUESTIONS

DO YOU HAVE ANY CONTROL OVER YOUR LIFE AND DESTINY? OR ARE YOU JUST A CONSEQUENCE OF WHAT IS ALREADY DESTINED FOR YOU?

The truth is ... YOU HAVE A CHOICE.

You always have a choice. To or <u>NOT</u> to think, feel, say, do, take action.

WHAT ARE YOU LOOKING FOR?

WHAT QUESTIONS IN LIFE ARE YOU LOOKING TO ANSWER?
WHAT SITUATION, ISSUE OR PROBLEM DO YOU WANT TO RESOLVE?

Are you one of those people who feel that life should be more? Do you feel like you are underachieving and unhappy? With your work, marriage or relationship, health or physique?

Do you feel like you have no purpose in life?

Do you find yourself reminiscing of those dreams you used to have when you were a child, teenager or young adult? Or even dreams you recently imagined, but found yourself immediately disregarding as impossible or even ridiculous?

Well, think again. With this book you will understand that all of your dreams are possible. There is nothing you cannot achieve. You can make anything happen. But most important of it all, that it is all within you to make them

23

real! You have everything you need, but you only need some help to see the tools you already have, in order to use them, take action and materialise all your dreams!

Action: Before you continue to read this book, I urge you to think of and write down at least 3 things – issues or challenges – or dreams that are in your mind right now that you can think of, that you want to resolve or change, and revisit these as you progress through the book – making notes or even adding as you find appropriate.

Tip: think of images to help you visualise and remember more easily.
I highly recommend you write them down using practical ways and high tech devices available, such as your Smartphone or pad you carry with you. Another possibility is white sheets of A4/3 paper place at home in visible places, such as the fridge or doors.

CHAPTER 2
THE BUILDING BLOCKS AND FOUNDATION

2.1 BUILDING BLOCKS

"Step by Step" ... "brick by brick" ...

I believe that a good way to building (or re-building) anything is more effective and solid if you do it in blocks; block-by-block, step-by-step. This approach helps you construct a solid foundation and base you can step, climb or lean on.

My friends say I am very practical in my way of thinking, and the people I work with tell me that I am really organised. So I guess I could say I have become like this in order to achieve what I need, some kind of project manager approach to life, where you need to understand your deliverables, dependencies between tasks and manage changes and contingencies in the best possible way.

I am rather more pop on my current list of role models, and amongst them I want to use Will Smith to start, quoting an example he uses in one of his interviews. When he was young, his Dad had a bakery and one day decided he wanted a new wall at the front of the shop. So he knocked the wall down and asked Will and his brother to re-build the wall. They had no skills but they built the wall every day for over 18 months until they finished. Will used to look at the wall and think that there was going to be a hole in the floor forever. But they did finish it and when they did, his father came and told them, **"Never tell me you can't do something"**.

This simple story has a lot more to what you can read at first. It involves commitment, learning, skills, practice, perseverance and patience, belief, and much more.

If there is one point I would like to highlight from this story, it is that all you need in life is to lay "one brick at a time", consistently, and you will achieve anything!

i) Vicious cycle or delicious cycle? (YIN & YANG)

In order to explain what is success – or at least how you could any where close to understand the concept and how to achieve it – let me start by explaining what is not and how we usually make sure not to be – or indeed feel – successful.

My best "coach" (that's my non-threatening term for Psychotherapist), tried to explained to me the concept so many times: **"the more you focus on the bad and negative, the worse you feel and the worse it gets"**. It is like a snowball. In fact, for over 5 years he told me this and didn't get it. I would have "reasons" to justify why it was so important to stick to my "values" and therefore feel upset about situations.

Now think about this as graphically as you can in a way that it works for you, I personally think of and use the yin-yang symbol. Imagining that every time you have a negative thought, the white half gets a round big black dot added on top. As you see it show up, you get upset and automatically another round big black appears on top of the white half, and so on. **It takes very little time for the white side to become ALL BLACK!**

This is how our brain works and the more you think black, the more black you see! **It is a vicious cycle!**

Now, if you can understand this point, try thinking if you do the exact opposite for every good thought, another good thought follows, and so on...

This is what successful people do! They think about good things, they focus on good things and what they want to do. They DO NOT all of the negative thoughts and bad things that can happen. And I tell you what, it usually works, and you know what happens if it doesn't, they think of something else to make it happen!

ii) Attitude
You often hear people talking about having the right "Attitude".

Let me summarise it for you: a **"happy, YES I CAN"** attitude is what will take you to conquer all that you dream of.

Nothing is certain, and most certain are that things will unfold in a different way from how you imagined the path would look like. But the result will be certain and you will achieve what you set yourself to do.

Forget for a moment about what people think, which is normally what stops you from being yourself and doing what you want. How would you prefer to see yourself from the outside, as a happy and positive person, fearless and driven, committed to deal with any challenges and deliver any tasks or action that are required to deliver a plan? Or as an unhappy, grumpy, negative person, who can see all the reasons why something won't work, shying away from responsibility and with no motivation to drive yourself – let alone others – to achieve anything?

Very simple Watson! The choice is YOURS!

iii) MOTIVATION vs. COMMITMENT over MOTIVATION (M/C/M)

I once attended a 1-day course to listen to and meet Dr. Steve Peters (psychiatrist). He is the man who helped Sir Chris Hoy and the Cycling Team GB achieved one of the most successful accolades of medals in the Olympics. He was appointed by UK Athletics to work with the country's high performance athletes after the 2012 Olympics.

If you think you have an over analytical and logical way of looking at problems, yet struggle with mood swings and outburst of anger, as well as points of what you would define as quasi madness, I would recommend you buy his book, "The chimp paradox". This will help you understand a very simplified model explaining the basics of your brain and how you manage your thoughts and most importantly, your feelings and behavioral reactions.

Back to the event: among the so many interesting facts and lessons I learnt that day, there was a point that Dr. Stevens highlighted, and it was the difference between "motivation & commitment".

He said **"you see, life is NOT about motivation ... it is about commitment"** and he went on to tell a story of a surgeon operating on an emergency patient at 2am in the morning, under hot and tiring conditions. This person could not stop operating and say: "I am tired and hot, I can't operate anymore, I am not motivated!"

This story stuck in my mind and made me realise for the first time the meaning of commitment and the power behind the word and the actions that followed.

You see, you could take that word and ask yourself the question, before you start any project, any relationship, or even every action.

28

I used to believe that WILL POWER was what made me achieve so many goals and successes in my short life, as well as overcome difficult times. But that day I realised it was my commitment to do all these things.

Furthermore, there is a strong thought behind the story and this concept: what if "your life depended on you operating on yourself?" Would you choose to feel motivated, or to be committed?

The choice is yours!

But as for me, I am committed to changing my life now! Are you?

iv) VALUES vs. Principles vs. VALUES
This is something that if you manage to understand and "re-wire" in your brain and beliefs (limiting beliefs), it will help you immensely.

This is another piece of the cornerstone of the tip of the iceberg that this book intends to share.

Values
Before you continue, stop for a minute and think about your values – no need to think as hard just yet – which you will need to write them down later in the book, in the self assessment section.

When we think about values, most of us think about words like honesty, loyalty, and others. They are intrinsic, subjective and very much rooted in our **subconscious minds,** and are said therefore to be difficult to modify.
Just to help you think of some, let us use for example, the English and history website lists the "9 English Values". You may identify yourself with some or have your own list.

1. Courage and selflessness
2. Truth
3. Honour
4. Fidelity
5. Discipline and Duty
6. Hospitality
7. Industriousness
8. Self-reliance
9. Perseverance

Principles
A principle is a **rule** that we have created to be able to live in society. It is external and more practical, and can supposedly be modify more easily.

Definitions of principles found in Wikipedia for example are:
- A descriptive comprehensive and fundamental law, doctrine, or assumption,
- A normative rule or code of conduct,

Values vs. principles
The best example I have heard to show the difference and application of these two concepts is that of a Gangster, where he/she has a set of values – like we all do – and a set of principles he applies to go about doing his business. However, he develops another set of principles in order to be able to live in society – and obviously not to get caught!

We all do this in one way or another to be able to be the best we can at what we want, so why not understand it and embrace it in order to consciously modify our principles to achieve our values in a way that is in less conflict with them.

Values AGAIN – Part II – A different approach or perspective
Now, I would like you to think of values in a different way.

Since we know that values are difficult to change, I thought that I was not going to be able to change anything in order to achieve what I wanted.

So then I came across Dr. John Demartini, and I had the opportunity to attend one of his presentations in person one Thursday summer night in a hotel in Knightsbridge, London.

During this presentation he started talking about Axiology – philosophical study of value from a good/right and beauty/harmony viewpoint and telos: which in summary is the end of purpose you subject yourself and your life to.

What I came to realise in this short presentation, is that if we focus on what we really want in life – our ultimate end and purpose – and are able to **rank it in terms of priorities** – a sort of hierarchy, we are able to make them our VALUES and identify more easily what is it that is important for us in life.

If we do this exercise, the immediate result is that we find a list of "Values" which we can actually change as much as we want – which is what happens as we grow up in any case.

You see, if you want to be somebody or have something, you can change your principles to obtain it, but it is only by understanding and changing your values that you will be able to keep it and sustain it over time.

For example:

You could create your list of values, for example, to set out to:

1. Look after your children
2. Look after your wife
3. Be the best at what you do – work, sport, etc.
4. [....]
5. [.....]
6. ....

Once you set your list of values / priorities, you will have to modify your principles, and ultimately your intrinsic values in order to achieve this.

People insist in saying that "People DO NOT Change" ... but you know what, that only is the case because "People DO NOT BELIEVE they CAN Change" or in other words ... "People DO NOT WANT to Change" ... "PEOPLE ARE IN GENERAL CHANGE AVERSE"

And you know what the interesting fact is ... **CHANGE IS THE ONLY CONSTANT IN LIFE!**

By the time you are finished with this book and you manage to understand yourself, you will be able not only to change but – as importantly – maintain these changes and achieve what you want in life.

NOTE: VALUES and RELATIONSHIPS
We underestimate the effect of values in relationships considerably. We underestimate how influenced we are by others and how much we are influencing people we relate to.

The key to managing and improving relationships starts with understating your values first and in parallel – if possible – the values of those you care and relate to for any reason. It is only in this way that we can keep our

32

independence – without giving up our end or purpose in life (Telos) – while respecting that of others.

(Telos): A telos (from the Greek τέλος for "end", "purpose", or "goal") is an end or purpose.

2.2 FOUNDATIONS

A couple of key points to start with

"All in your life is right and is just the way it is supposed to be and the way you asked for".

JP TI

"Whether you think you can, or you think you can't--you're right."

Henry Ford

The following are some key aspects, subjects, and considerations for you to keep in mind throughout the book:

A – REALISE
i) Your current life situation DOES NOT EQUAL your WHOLE LIFE
The current situation you are living today is a specific moment in time. It is the result of a combination of results, which derived from a mix of conscious and subconscious decisions you have made over time, over the years. The interesting truth is that your life situation today DOES NOT equal your whole life. What is happening to you right now, be it the current job you have or don't have, the family, the friends, the car, everything is just a situation.

There are so many examples I could use to show you how people mistakenly confuse their situation with their lives:

One simple example we can use is when people lose their jobs. The whole world seems to fall apart, especially if they are deep in the rat race and have no savings to rely upon to get through the period while they try to find another job. Once they lose the job, people forget it is just one occurrence, one moment in time and they project their life on to that job. People then tend to think and, therefore feel, that their whole life is over. People usually identify themselves with their roles and the status it gives them among various other qualifications. The problem resides in the loss of identity, and remembering that the job does not make them as a person, and they are still the same person, with the same qualifications and skills. People end up beating themselves up or blaming others, or their past, family and partners in order to find a reason (or excuse).

Something similar may happen to people when they get divorced too.

Other simpler examples are all those moments when we make simple mistakes, like breaking a glass, or spilling some coffee on our clothes, and immediately call ourselves rude names such as idiot, stupid, useless, etc. We effectively create a generalisation to define ourselves based on one single event or mistake. Once you realise what the formula for happiness and success is, you will realise that sometimes these "accidents" are in fact signs and have other meanings, which if we learn to be aware enough, are there to show us or help us in other ways.

Action: write down what you think is your "life" right now, and try to work out what you think is only a situation and what you "think" is your whole life.

ii) A dot in a piece of paper
The previous point about life situations can be put into perspective with the following exercise:

Start by imagining a huge piece of white paper, or try grabbing and A3 or A4 piece of paper. Then imagine or just put a simple black pen dot on the piece of paper.

Now look at that dot or spot.

Now if you think of yourself in the context of the world population, 7+bn people, you are that dot.
If you think of that dot as every event in your life, how relevant is an event in a lifetime? People say that the only things you can't escape are death and taxes, all the rest ... well ... is just a dot! ☺

What I am trying to say is that nothing will really impact in your life significantly, unless you let the dot become your whole life.

•

B - IMAGINE
Imagination! Is the most powerful tool we posses, that we own! It is free and allows us to be whomever we want to be, take us wherever we want to go, have anything we want to have ... with just one thought!

iii) Life is the effect and result of what you think
You are the creator of your life, every day, every minute ... every step, every action, every person you choose to relate to ... you are the creator of your life ... you are the creator of your own destiny!

Everything in your life is what you have asked for... it is exactly what you want: where you live, where you studied, who you hang out with, where you go for tea, coffee, to drink, to the cinema, to the pub, dancing, shopping ... everything you do and experience is exactly what you want.

iv) What is in it for you? ... visualise!
It is so important to visualise. If you think that all that you have in your life is exactly what you wanted. Everything you have, you actually thought about having it in one way or another. What do you think you need to do in order to have what you want going forward? Exactly! Imagine! Visualise!

All you need to do is think about what you want, write it down, and imagine you already have it. But you need to feel it as if it is real, like you have the job, you are driving that car, you win that championship, whatever it is you want ... you need to feel like you have it right now, at this very moment.

The limbic system in your brain does not know if it is real or not.

To complete what is required in order to emit the right signal to your subconscious mind, it is recommended that you also add movement when you imagine and feel.

So come on! Close your eyes and do it ... what is it going to be? Would you like to have that new job? Or own a yacht one day? Close your eyes, breathe deep, and imagine yourself sailing in your new yacht in the Mediterranean.

C – PLAY TO DEFINE
Next, I use two examples that resonate with the way I used to look at life, which are representative of my own habits. Please use these if they work for you or think of the ones that represent you better and help you re-define and switch yourself to the positive side.

36

v) A 'what if' person
Are you a "what if" type of person?

Some people are excellent at finding the reason why something cannot work. These are called "what if" type of people. Sometimes they project this on other people, sometimes just to themselves, but rest assured they do it most of the time.

Are you one of them? This is an "attitude" and a "habit" which affects all that you do and most likely those around you that trust you. But do not worry, you can change this. And if you do not want to, it is ok, but just be aware and at least try **NOT** to do it to other people.

The point here is that happy and successful people are not this way. They do not think about what can go wrong. They either firmly believe that it will be alright or they just find the solution to the problem or challenge.

vi) Half empty / half full glass person ... or why is it not full?
Are you a half empty or a half full glass type of person? I used to think I was the latter, always trying to be happy and jovial with people. People would even tell me I was such a positive person. But it was not until this year I finally realised I was the former. I would always be looking at the glass and thinking why is it not full? This in reality it the same as seeing it half empty!
I would constantly be looking at what was missing, what was wrong, what I didn't have. **Or I would keep changing the size of the glass so I could never fill it up :-)**

D – UNDERSTAND
vii) Success and failure

"Success is the progressive realisation of a worthy idea."
Earl Nightingale

Failure and success ... success and failure ... go hand in hand. It was not again until this year when I finally understood this relationship, and the benefits associated to it.

I was listening to one of the many inspirational talks from another very successful person on YouTube when I realised all the skills I had. Skills, you may ask? Yes, skills. It was when I realised all I had learnt thanks to my previous experiences, of which many resulted in failures. But what I had also failed to realise in the past was that for every experience, for every failure, I had gained something – a lesson, a skill, a contact – and I had also failed to capitalise on this, as I insisted in trying to forget about the event because of the "negative" association I would attach to it.

It was one summer night that I took a piece of paper and for the first time I listed – proudly – all my failures! And next to each one I noted what I had gained from them. And the best of all is that I ultimately was able to see my successes – my achievements – for what they are, for what I set my self to do before I made it happen and not in comparison with somebody else's achievements.

Action: if you dare to accept yourself for who you are and are ready and willing to praise yourself for what you have achieved, please write down all your failure and successes, and try to see if you can appreciate all that you are.

*Important: Please understand that it is ok not to want to achieve, but it is important to understand that we cannot expect to be high achievers if a) we are not, b) We chose **Not** to take actions and do what is needed. The key here is to accept yourself, but before you do that, you need to learn about yourself.*

Note: do remember, that if you are taking actions and you are not getting the results you want, you need to change your actions!

vii) 80 Percent – The power of consistency and persistence

80 % is showing up: some of the most successful people quote that 80% of success is just showing up. You could translate it into **consistency or persistency**, but the point is that you have to be present in order to make things happen.

This is something I learnt while exercising and then realised I had been doing it for years in my every day life. Consistency always delivers results! Just showing up and doing as many sets and reps as I could manage will reap results, no matter how I feel, no matter what I think!

Even if you didn't have all the time you required to prepare, you will always be able to achieve something –

even if it is an action and follow up session or meeting. At least, you will be a bit closer to your goal!

Remember, get up, get dressed, put your smile on ... and show up!!!

"Practice makes perfect"

Please do not get me wrong, of course I have some days than are better than others. It is after all like anything you do in life, a job, a sport, exercising ... you need to PRACTICE! You need to have as much consistency as possible, and create and practice the new habits you develop for yourself, based on the foundations, values, beliefs, principles, vision you have set yourself.

viii) Repeat ...

There is a very simple process that we carry out almost instinctively after breathing, or that we build in our daily plan, but somehow take for granted and many times fail to follow properly, with detrimental effects to our health and the way we manage our emotions and ourselves. The stages of this process are very simple and easy to follow, yet sometimes we disregard them or subordinated in an unbalanced manner.

These stages are:
1. Rest (be re-born, rejuvenate and relax)
2. Eat (put fuel and nourish)
3. Exercise (grow, replenish and get stronger)
4. Work (think, feel and create)
5. Repeat ...

More detail under the Health (& Exercise) in section 7.

CHAPTER 3
LEARNING ABOUT YOURSELF

Following on nicely from success and failure, please spend 5 to 10 mins doing the quick self assessments to help start understanding yourself:

Please do not underestimate the importance of this section. Even if you think you know yourself, I would assume you are reading this book because there is something else you want to understand about you, or change, or improve.

Do you have a balanced life? Do you know what your values are? Your priorities? What is important to you? And most importantly, are they aligned to each other and your actions?

PRIORITIES   LIFE

3.1 SELF ASSESSMENT
Your perspective on your own life – Understanding and getting to know yourself

Well, I want you to think about your current situation as of today, and simply answer the following question:

PART I
I) CURRENT SITUATION: using a scale of 1 to 5, where:
1 is terrible
2 is bad
3 is ok
4 is good
5 is amazing

First time: answer the following questions

How happy are you?

1   2   3   4   5

How successful do you think you are?

1   2   3   4   5

Interestingly enough, if you write down all the things you had set yourself to do in order to give yourself the title of successful [x] number of years ago. Perhaps try to answer the questions again and see how you feel about it.

Most of us will find that we have achieved what we set ourselves to do, and we had initially set these goals, most of us would have said that if we had achieved said goal we would be happy. But what happened? We moved the boundaries further and further and we started comparing ourselves to others and use their "standards" to judge our success. Now, how do you think this affects your so-called "happiness"? You guessed it right: not too positively, affecting our self-confidence, belief, and faith.

Second time: So now I'll ask you to answer the questions for a second time.

CURRENT SITUATION vs. YOUR WHOLE LIFE
You would also recall the section where we talked about your life situation vs. your whole life.

Third time: So now I ask you again to answer the questions for a third time.

How happy are you?

1   2   3   4   5

How successful do you think you are?

1   2   3   4   5

Could you please compare your grading and see how much your perception of yourself has changed simply through adding a little perspective?

ii) Priorities 1-10

Please use the list below to prioritise what is important in your life. Use the list as an indicative starting point and feel free to add any extra ones or ignore those included as you find appropriate:

O - Life in general
O - Health
O - Food
O - Family
O - Relationships
O - Friends
O - Work
O - Stress
O - Money
O - Children (if applicable)

iii) DRIVERS

These are the deep internal forces that drive us to do what we do, they shape us and create habits which we use to make us or break us.

I would like to use Anthony Robbins list of drivers to start this section. Tony says that everyone is driven by one or more of the following drivers:

- Certainty
- Variety (uncertainty)
- Significance
- Connection and Love
- Contribution
- Growth

I will not attempt to copy his definitions, but try to explain what I understand and how I have used it to understand myself and my behaviour.

I have to be honest to say that I have known about this for quite some time, since I started listening to Tony's audio CDs many years ago. But the challenge I had then is that I did not really understand it and how the human mind and the basic laws of the universe relate to each other to support and work together to affect my thoughts, feelings and actions.

Long story short, through looking back at my behaviour and my life, I have finally come to realise that the biggest driver in my life is **"Connection and Love"**. I have always "wanted and needed" this, and in my case, I would look to fulfil it with relationships with partners and friends, externally.

Now, the magic of learning has showed me that if I want to feel love, I can do that in a "heartbeat" – like Tony says – by simply thinking and feeling it in my mind. Or if I want to feel love, I can feel it by giving love to others. If you want to feel love … give love! You will feel it immediately.

Understanding myself and the tools I can use to help me fulfil what drives me in life is priceless, as I can now manage my feelings better.
The reason why I tell you this is because I want you to look at these drivers and think what is the most important one for you. You may need to play with them for a while to

understand what is it that you are "craving" for most of the time.

If you can work out what drives you in life, you will be able to look at your own foundations and where you need to start. This will allow you to work out the means to fulfil it, as well as plans and strategies to deal with them so it can affect the rest of your life in a positive way.

With all of the above in mind ... and please do follow the cycle and process proposed ...

In terms of steps, as an initial action, the following are ways in which you can think in general terms in order to align all your thoughts:
1. Priorities
2. Wishes
3. What do you love doing?
4. Values
5. Perceptions
6. Vision
7. Mission, purpose and meaning of life

3.2 ASK YOURSELF SOME CRUCIAL QUESTIONS

I would like you now to start thinking and answering to yourself some very crucial questions that will help you to change your life.

To answer these questions you can simply take two different approaches

APPROACH 1: Use a white piece of paper, A3 if you have it to hand, or any note pad, or your phone, and write down anything that comes to mind for each question for 2 to 5 minutes ... or

APPROACH 2: You can ask somebody else to do this for you! Some of us find it hard to assess ourselves, as we struggle to take control over our lives. But this is ok. A friend can help, but remember that only you have a PhD on yourself! Nobody knows you the way you do!

i) What do you want to do?
First, take 2 minutes right now and write down all of the things you love doing, all of the things you would like to do and all the things you would like to become!!!

Ready? GO!!!

Now, take 2 mins to write down all the things that you wanted to be when you were younger.

Note: If you are a student at high school or university, write down all the things you were dreaming of doing or becoming 3-5 years ago.

Ready? GO!!!

ii) Who are you? What are your values? Who would you like to be or be seen as? What are your highest priorities and most important parts and people in your life?

Action: using a piece of paper please make a list of these and draw a line in the middle from top to bottom and using two columns write down:

On the left, all you would like to be as a person – think about the values you want to represent and your highest priorities you ranked on the previous exercise. Think about who you want to be rather who you think you are. The reason why I asked you this is because what you write is actually who you are, and the only reason why you are not or don't behave is because your subconscious mind takes over, or as it also known ... "the chimp". You may want to read Dr. Stevens Peters' book the Chimp Paradox to fully understand, but in my summary understanding is because your emotional side takes over and does not allow you to believe and behave in the way you want to.

On the right, what you would like to have in achievements or more material items.

iii) What is your vision? Is it aligned to your values?
Do you have a mission? What is your purpose and the meaning of your life? For example, for me it is to be the happiest and most influential in my own life and help as many people as possible to have a better life and make their dreams come true.

iv) What is your purpose in life?

What do you want to achieve: in relationships, jobs, financially, in every aspect of your life?

Final action: once you have answered the questions - in order to help you visualise and focus your subconscious mind to start creating the life of your dreams - I recommend you **write down the purpose of your live, based on your vision and values, with a define deadline and what you are going to give to people in order to achieve this.**

Note: also see the PVSPPA model at the end of chapter 6.

3.3 FINDING YOUR SKILLS AND STRENGTHS

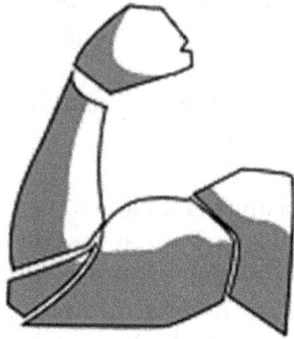

One key building block to increasing your self-confidence and to believe is to work out and be aware of your skills and strengths.

I know you may think you have none or you have them all, but from personal experience and observation of others, I know this is usually skewed towards a distorted view of reality. This may be for better or worse – or a negative appreciation of yourself due to our tendency to compare ourselves to others – and using what I call other people's "Rulers" to measure your own life and achievements.

A good and funny example I have found is when watching an episode of the TV programme called the "The Apprentice", where you would find a contestant making a statement with tremendous confidence: "I am really good at selling and dealing with people"... then at the next task, we would find out that the contestant is not able to sell nor liaise with people at all! Even worse, having finished the task, most times you would find the person has not understood his limitations, continuing to be in denial, and blaming others for his failings! Do you know anyone that behaves like this, maybe a very close person to you?

I believe that finding your own skills and strengths is very important, in many more ways than just feeling good about yourself. If you are like most people in this world, where negatives thoughts just appear in your head, especially to insult yourself, calling your self (and others) names such as stupid, slow, and more? The bad news is this is just a **HABIT** that you develop and practice on a daily basis. But the good news is that you can switch it to the opposite. This will not only help you **FOCUS** on what is important and positive, but will simply help you get on with your days at peace with yourself.

To start with, there is a fantastic phrase I picked up for the fitness training programme P90X – **"Do your best ... forget the rest"**.

The point we all fail to understand is that most of us always try our best. If we don't, it is normally because WE CANNOT. What I have come to learn is that if we CANNOT, it is either by: 1) Choice: which is in fact a completely valid choice, and then you have to learn to accept it and live with it and the consequences, or 2) We do not know a better way! This is where I think that this book will help many of us learn better ways to manage ourselves to truly achieve our FULL POTENTIAL!!

Most of us dwell on the fact that we have "No qualifications", or "No successes or track record", or we "Don't know how to ...", but the fact is that this 1) does not always matter, as we all have a love for something and are good at something – the key is learning to stop bullying ourselves and learn to 2) create a list of all the "Successes & failures" we have achieved over the years. Yes, failures too, to learn to appreciate ourselves.

Action: split a piece of paper into 4 columns, in column 1 write down your successes, in column 3 write down your failures, now in columns 2 & 4, next to what you wrote in

1&3, write down what you did wrong, learn or showed as a skilled in each one of the cases. You see, what you are writing down in columns 2&4 are the "Lessons" you learnt with each experience and this are in fact "Skills" you have developed.

I came up with this simple exercise while listening to John Asaraff one day on YouTube at midnight on a summer's day. He was going on about how he thought he had no skills; he didn't know anything about Finance, Marketing or Law! And I thought, wait a minute, I know about all of that. He went on to say how at one point he realised how he was good at talking to people, networking and talking in public! So I thought, wait a minute I am good at that too! But the silliest thing is that until that night, all I could think of was what I didn't have, what I didn't know, what I was missing.

The conclusion I came to at that moment and over the coming days is that if I concentrate on learning what I am good at, I simply feel better about myself and then I can focus in finding a way to get better at what I want to develop. Also, I realised that I can always hire people that are good at what I am not, because there are specialists at everything and people that are naturally better than me at certain things. Why would I want to force myself to be a lion, when I am a tiger?

Another way to look at your strengths is by looking back at all the challenges you have faced in your life and how you managed to overcome them. I'll leave you to think about that.

KNOWING WHO TO TALK TO
I used to avoid doing certain things in life, especially those I didn't feel qualified or an expert at doing. It was not until very recently that I understood the skill of "knowing who to talk to".

Whether it's accounting, finance, law, marketing, whatever it is you think you need help with, there is always an expert. And the best thing is that they are all willing and able to help, and the best part is that people love being asked for help.

Now, I would like to quickly mention some of the key lessons you will learn in the next sections, including: attraction, abundance, love. They all come together to help you find the right person and part from your money to pay for the service received, as it will be returned to you with interest!

COMPOUNDING
Taking into consideration your "strengths" and "knowing who to talk to", and of course the various sections and lessons including in this book, I want to share with you a very powerful concept – a tool, that you can make a "habit" – that will help you immensely in the process of achieving anything you set yourself to do or become.

This is what I refer to as "Compounding".

There are several ways to explain it, but in simple terms it refers to the consistent and continuous habit of taking actions, everyday, every week, every year! Your whole life!

I have taken this concept from two main areas of my life, Finance and the Gym. To explain it, there a couple of simple examples we can use;

Finance: if you put £10 in the bank and receive 10% every year, you get £1 after year one, then you add both and you have £11, so next year you get £1.1 and so on every year.

Gym: even if you train 3-5 days a week, while having a reasonable nutrition plan, you will get fitter and/or build muscle – no matter what! I have personally grown ~70kg up to ~89kg healthier – some stages a bit leaner than others – in a matter of a couple of years. All you need is show up and run, lift, jump – whatever is you enjoy – and you will improve every time, building on whatever you did the day before, the week before... Compounding every rep! Compounding every session, every day!

Finally, there is one more example which I really like that explains the simplicity of compounding. This example is about travelling from one city to another. Let's say that you live in London and would like to go to Brighton, in the south coast. In order to do this you could use various means to get there. You could go by helicopter, car, motorbike, bicycle, etc. Alternatively, you could just WALK. If you walk, just a little bit everyday, you will get there eventually. Now, this example may need the assumption that you have set yourself a clear goal, that you have chosen the right paths and roads, and that you are checking your progress as you go along. But the fact is that if you take even just a couple of steps consistently, you will get there. Compounding step by step! Compounding all the way!

Action: So now you can start compounding on your strengths, you can compound on things you want to get better at, or you can compound by contacting the people you need to partner with or hire.
The same can be applied to your whole life – family, relationships, work, projects, businesses, hobbies ... – and as long as you "Compound", you will achieve anything you set yourself to do or become! Guaranteed!

So ... start "COMPOUNDING" ... right NOW!
Day-by-day ... £ by £ ... rep by rep ... step by step!
All you need to do is ... start and ... COMPOUND!

CHAPTER 4
WORK SMART AND BE EFFECTIVE

"Don't ONLY work HARD ... You need to Work SMART and BELIEVE"

Fact of life: Successful people focus on what is important!

One of the things that we all are told during our lives is that you only make things happen if you work hard.

The problem with this statement and the concept is that there is no relative side to it or qualitative angle to the work you need to do.

Therefore, people confuse the statement with putting long hours, or having the longest list of activities to go through in a day, which by the way, we normally never get through – as it is not humanly impossible to achieve - and then beat ourselves up for no working hard enough and not achieving. Does this resonate with you at all? ☺

Although I am a strong believer in the need to work to achieve things in life, understating that nothing comes easy, and even if you are lucky enough to get a lucky strike, you still need to know a way to keep and maintain what came to you so "easily".

Shortcuts do not usually work, and most of the time the results obtained is short lived.

I have worked very hard in life to achieve all that I am, but I now realise I partially failed in two very important aspects. One of them is that I doubted myself and consequently failed to fully BELIEVE in what I was trying to achieve, resulting in giving up many of the various initiatives and dreams I have had in my life. The other aspect I failed to fully grasp was the concept of working SMART. This is not just about having a specific set to SMART goals, but about understanding exactly what is the best way to prioritise my efforts in order to get to the desired result in the most EFFECTIVE manner.

It was because of my continuous desire to make myself more effective, while feeling that I was not getting the best results, that I came across the quadrants of effectiveness shown in a couple of books and I finally understood what I needed to do.

- Do you procrastinate?
- Do you take control of life or feel that life controls you?
- Do you end the days filling fulfilled and with a sense of achievement? Or feel you didn't do enough, beat your self up and feel like you're underachieving?

I have been there, done that, bought the t-shirt and went out to drink or back home to watch TV till past midnight too! ... ☺

If I had to recommend the best way to prioritise your tasks and actions, I would just say ... do what is really important and aligned to your priorities first, led by your inner self and gut feelings.

Now, if you would like to understand a bit more on how you could structure and change the way you do things currently, below is my interpretation and a view on prioritising actions you can take when planning your day, your week, your projects, and your life!

Note: I saw this concept in at least two books, and learnt from them, the most notorious being "the 7 habits of effective people", by Stephen R. Covey. I recommend this book, but this is my interpretation and personal definitions for actions.

4.1 TYPES OF ACTIONS

ACTION 1 – Important/NOT Urgent
[LIFE CHANGING – Decide **WHEN**]

ACTION 2 – Important/urgent
[REQUIRED – DO IT **NOW**]

ACTION 3 – NOT Important/Urgent
[MANAGEABLE – **DELEGATE**]

ACTION 4 – NOT Important/NOT Urgent
[IRRELEVANT – **LATER**]

In my own words, based on my interpretations and life experiences, I would define these actions as follows:

Action 1: Important and NOT Urgent
This is the most important and defining action you will take in your life, as it will potentially affect the course it will take in many more ways than you realise. However, this is the one we all tend to disregard, leave for last, and most time never get around to doing. Amazingly, this is the one that if we do not do, we end up doing what is important for others and living a life defined by consequences, feeling we have no control over our lives and that things just happened to us! We would rather watch TV, go somewhere, have a cup of tea, or find anything to do rather than do it. Say hello to our friend, procrastination! (See action 4)

Key step: in order to take these actions, you need to **make sure you put a deadline to it, allocate time and schedule it.**

Action 2: Important and Urgent

This is the type of action we cannot put off, as they need to be dealt with immediately. By dealing with them, we make sure that our day has no negative consequences in the short and long term and therefore affect how we deal with the other actions. Some examples of this type could be a client call to make a complaint, or a shipment that has not arrived, or a simple accident that we need to clean up after.

Key step: deal with them as soon and fast as possible.

Action 3: NOT Important and Urgent

This is the one we spend a considerable amount of time during the day. I heard one time a person using the example of M&Ms, Managers & (e)mails. Managers approach us with all sorts of requests, many of which as not really urgent or could be placed in the list of actions to be dealt with after dealing with Actions 1 & 2. Another tendency many people create is that of trying to reply and organise each and every email they receive, which ends up consuming their day with not much achieved at the end of it.

Key step: the recommendations to deal with this, is to **learn to say NO!** And **learn to manage up!** Making managers and colleagues, friends & family, understand the impact it will have in your other work if you have to drop everything to deal with their requirement. If it is really important, it will then move up to action 2, if not, it will be degraded to action 4.

Action 4: NOT Important and NOT Urgent

(sigh) ... many people's favourite! And most times taking the shape of "procrastination" and finding any activity to do instead of what really needs to be done.

But please do not assume I think these are completely unnecessary from a personal point of view. If managed properly, procrastination is as important to help you relax and take your mind off things.

You can find yourself doing it without even noticing. But until you become aware, it will be hard to realise how to organise yourself in order to do and achieve what you really want.

Key step: the most important point here is not to focus on realising how and when you procrastinate, but rather focus on what you in order to keep your focus on what is important and what will make a difference to you, your life, and your happiness.

CHAPTER 5
THE BASICS

In this paramount section, I need you to try and just read the concepts without making an initial judgement. You can come back again and judge everything I share and laugh at it if you **choose** to.

I think, I feel, I believe ...

These basic concepts are some of the most important BLOCKS of the universe and how life works. I do not intend for you to believe in everything I say, word for word. In fact, there is no way you will believe in anything you do not want to believe. However, if you choose to believe, sustain positivity, and consequently attempt new experiences in your own life, I can assure you that it will change it forever, like mine did. These pillars give you the foundation to do and build anything you set yourself to become.

Understanding and consistently applying these BLOCKS, will help you become a MASTER of your own MIND and will allow you to transform your life completely. You will become increasingly aware and able to change the way you look at things with 180 degrees difference, and then 360 degrees as a new reborn you.

THE CHANGE WILL BE HUGE!

Note: most of the basics are based on the various books I have read and people I have listened to over the years, and some key ones during the last year.

It is also worth highlighting is that although I had been a person almost obsessed with "Perfection", so much so that I used to say "I study and practice Peak Performance".

Then one day I realised we are actually all PERFECT! And it is by realising this to start with that you can achieve the peak! But in order to be able to do this, there are some very BASIC concepts that need to need to be learnt and understood.

So I would like to start with some concepts that I believe are key and will help you as much as they have helped me:

1. Limiting Believes
2. Habits
3. Time

5.1 LIMITING BELIEVES

"Whether you think you can, or you think you can't--you're right."

Henry Ford

This is the one point that explains why we set ourselves to do less that we can, achieve less that what we dream, and settle for even less than we think we deserve. We have "limiting believes" that have been passed on to us and into our brain.

Depending on the education, parents and people we have related to during the years – among many other things, these believes have been taught to us, growing and accumulating, shaping the way we act and the things you set to do and become.

How many times we heard people say: "Oh, you can't do that, you can't do such sport, you can't sing, you can't dance, you can't act, etc."

We learn to accept from a young age, that there are limitations to what we can do and become. People usually learn and use all sorts of reasons (excuses) to rationalise and justify why is not possible, be it background, ethnicity, location, money, etc.

I am sure that once upon a time you used to dream and believe you could do anything in life, and slowly but surely, you started putting aside those dreams while focusing on what you could not do.

The good news for you is ... you do not need to maintain these limiting believes! You do not even need to change them! All you need to do is start again, and think of all the things you would like to do.
Make sure you use the HIGHER FACULTIES OF YOUR BRAIN to create all and everything you want!

Tip: every time you hear the voice in your head telling you can't do something, just focus on what you want to do ... and believe!

Conscious vs. subconscious mind ... and body

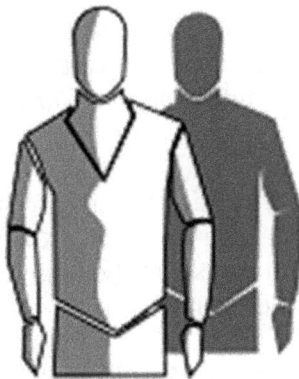

It's so important to be able to distinguish between the conscious and sub-conscious mind, as it will be help you manage and choose the way you act and react to situations and life in general.

The conscious mind is our thinking, educated mind, which we can use to accept or reject what we think and do.

The subconscious mind is our emotional mind. There is no choice for us and we must accept and cannot reject the situation, and cannot divide between realities.

- The subconscious mind tells you WHO you are.
- The conscious mind tells you WHAT you know.
- You hear with your ears.
- You listen with you emotions.

5.2 HABITS

Repetition is the master of skill, but if you keep doing the same and is not working... you will keep getting the same results.

A habit is an idea fixed in your subconscious mind. A habit is the external and ultimate representation of who we really are.

"Any idea that is held in the mind that is either feared or revered will begin at once to clothe itself in the most convenient and appropriate physical forms available."
Andrew Carnegie

In order to change, you need to follow a system, where you make a decision → give yourself a command → change your habits → and consistently apply yourself through actions to change the results.

The paradigm we face as thinking human beings is the fact that we continuously "battle" between the decisions and actions we make with our conscious mind and what we think with our subconscious mind.

The key to managing yourself and especially any behaviour that is unhelpful for your ultimate goals in life is the sub-conscious mind.

By understanding some key concepts and rules on how life, the brain and the universe work, we are able to effectively start "resetting" or "re-programming our subconscious mind in order for it to align with our conscious mind.

5.3 THE CONCEPT OF TIME

How long is a piece of string? Well, there's no need to answer, as there is no answer.

The same applies to time: what is time? Again, no need to answer, as there is no answer.

Time does not exist. You cannot see it. You cannot keep it.

∞

What I am trying to tell you is that all you have to work on in life is this very moment. What happened yesterday is the past, and there is nothing you can do to change it. What will happen tomorrow has not yet occurred, but you may be able to influence it, but you can only do that with your actions in this very moment.

Eckhart Tolle talks about this in his book **"The Power of Now"**, where he talks about **"Mind & Clock time"**. In summary, the past and the future are only in your mind – **Mind time** – while the now is the only time you can influence directly as it is happening at this very moment – **Clock time**.

You need to focus on the moment, and live in the moment, as you can only influence your thoughts and actions as you bring them and they come to your mind.

The Importance of the Now – This is more than just a concept: Every day focus on the moment, the "now"; focus on what you can control. Focusing on either the past or the future will bring no further immediate benefit or results to your life. There are many phrases you will find in books and the internet, but in summary, we need the past to learn form it, the future to aim and look forward to it – dream, get excited, visualise, feel – the present, the moment, the now, to act and make a difference.

There is so much to write about this rule and principle of life, but in fact there is one book that goes into detail at length. If you would like to dig deeper into this concept, I recommend you read or listen to "The Power of Now" by Eckhart Tolle.

CHAPTER 6
UNIVERSAL LAWS

We have one infinite power. The natural laws of the universe have helped us shape the world we live in today. The people that have achieved the most incredible achievements in the world are using these rules naturally.

At last I've learnt these rules! And I want to share them with you!

The irony is you don't actually need to learn this rules because you already know them. It is just a case of becoming aware of them.

6.1 THE MAIN LAWS

I would say that there are 3 main laws that you can focus on in order to help you achieve your dreams and a fulfilling/successful life by your definition. These are LOVE, ATTRACTION, and ABUNDANCE, which are all interrelated.

LOVE

Love is the most powerful force and energy there is in this world and the universe.

But you need to start by loving YOU ... if you do not love yourself, it makes it harder (and some times practically impossible) to love someone else.

This is why it is so important to look after yourself and your needs first, in order to feel good and then be able to look after others.

Many people try to live their lives by loving others in an attempt to feel love and be loved. The problem with this approach is that the pillars and foundations are being based outside of our heart and bodies. Imagine how would you be able to build a house if your foundations are in a different plot of land? Think about it.

It's easy to get confused and think that we are endorsing selfishness when we are in actual fact, referring to appreciation. Understanding what is special about you, all of the great qualities you have and believe in and apply through your behaviour and the way you treat others.

There is a book by Louise L. Hay called 'You Can Heal Yourself'. It asks you in one of the chapters to think of yourself as a child. You would treat a child with love and care, right? Or if you were a child, how would you like to be treated and spoken to. Well, you can do that right now and onwards. You would never call a child stupid! Would you? You would never be nasty! Call them names! Tell them they are good for nothing and discourage them on their attempts to do or achieve something! Would you? So why would you do that to yourself? Something to think about,...right?

Love yourself ... as if you were that child!

Love: How many times do we hear the phrase, "YOU don't know what love is"?

A friend of mine told me this one day over a phone call, the same friend that recommended the book to me. And you know what? I didn't like it, but as I was going through my life changing process, I gave her the benefit of the doubt. And it was when one day I finally realised how I was treating myself, how I was talking to myself, let alone others, that I understood that I did not love myself. I understood I really did not know how to love.

I dare you to listen to yourself and look into the way you treat yourself and others, and ask the question: "Do I know what Love is?" ☺

Now, once you are capable to love yourself, which is indeed very hard for many of us, you can start focusing on giving love. And as you start giving, you will immediately receive love, you will feel it and you will receive it from others. This is a result of the **law of attraction.**

LAW OF ATTRACTION
Whatever you think ... you are right!

What you think, you will attract. The brain does not differentiate between reality and imagination. Whatever you think about and focus on becomes reality to your brain, and with this comes the feelings too.

Your thoughts would then emit an energetic frequency which is picked up by those same thoughts in real life: the family, the wife, the children, the job, the friends, the house, the car and so on.

You attract everything in your life and you do this through what you think, as simple as that.

This is the most basic rule that rules our lives. Make sure you understand it, because with this rule you will be able to transform your life completely.

The clothes you are wearing, the people you hang out with, the place where you live, the course you are studying, your current and previous jobs, your current and previous relationships ... you have attracted all this with the power of your thoughts.

The simplest and best graphical example we can use to represent the law of attraction is the one used in the book

'The Secret'. Imagine you are like a TV company tower, sending signals for each channel (thought and wish) you have. This signal is then picked up by the TVs in exactly the same channel.

So ...

Live Life to the Full: One of the most important gifts we have been given is "Life". One of the questions people ask themselves every day is, how do I live life to the full? Or especially on their death bed, most people ask themselves ... did I live a full life?

One of the decisions we need to make is to love life, to be alive, to live to the full. And how do you do this? The answer is much simpler than you realise ... **LOVE what you do! Everything you do! ... And most importantly, do the things you LOVE!**

When you see children, with no worries and responsibilities, they wake up every morning looking forward to the moment, what they are doing now, trying to play all the time, role play, using their imagination ...

Do you remember how you used to feel when you were a child? Well, try to do the same now. Wake up every morning as if you were going out to play, or as if you are going on holidays or to a trip you wanted to go to all year.

The way you live life every day, every moment, will define what your day is like and most importantly, will define what your life is going forward – your tomorrow, your future, your goals and dreams – and you will attract more of it ...

Be Grateful: Gratitude is what I would call the "**antidote**" to all bad feelings. If you think about the things you are grateful for, and keep focusing on them, all bad feelings will simply disappear. This is because you cannot have bad feelings if you are thinking of good feelings.

Think about anything in your life you are thankful and grateful for. You can simply start with your body, the most amazing machine in existence in this world. It is unique and it is all yours!
You can be grateful for your health, and for everything and anything to do with yourself.

You can be grateful for other people in your life, your parents, siblings, children, if you have any.

You can be grateful for your friends, colleagues or just people you bump into that are nice to you, such as service desks, tills attendants at the shops, anyone !

You can be grateful about the past, the present and the future. Yes, the future! Think about the things you want in the future and be grateful now! As if you have them already! And ... you guessed it ... you will attract more of it!

Action: the best way to start and end a day is by being grateful. The happiest and most successful people tend to have a habit where they go through what they are grateful for as soon as they open their eyes and get out of bed. They also carry out a similar exercise as they prepare themselves to go to bed. At the same time, they aim to be aware and be grateful of their experiences throughout the day, being thankful for everything that is right and the kindness of the people around them.

Tip: Use the following affirmation,

"I am grateful that ... "

Appreciate and embrace: No matter what you decide to do or become in life, the key is to appreciate and embrace who you are and what you have.

The key point about this, coupled with gratitude, is to realise that the more you take **"ownership"** and **"responsibility"**, the more you take control of your life, and the more you focus on appreciating your life and the more you will feel positive, the more you are able to get in the right mindset in order to make any changes that are needed to achieve what you desire or want to change.

Just remember that until now you have done the best you can, and if so, this is the most you could have done to date. So why be harsh on yourself?

There is no need to think about the past, what you have not done, what you are not, what you do not have, because all these thoughts would just bring you down.

Ultimately, it is your decision to do what you do, to be in the situation you are. You can change it, with vision, a plan, and consistent actions.

So in the interim, appreciate what you have and who you are, and embrace the situation and each moment in your life, changing them as necessary if you want to change the way you feel.

Focus – "Remember to FOCUS": To keep your **focus** consistently and building your own set of habits and goals is what will make you and keep you happy and successful in whatever you want to do and be in life.

Your thoughts towards things that make you happy: people, dreams, actions and objects that excite you, are all within a framework that helps you move forward.

If there is one action you can take each day, during the whole day, to be able to change your focus towards what makes you feel good... Do it! You can make that change!

Action: whenever you're thinking about something negative, at that very moment, think about exactly the opposite! This will give you the chance to go into your thoughts and allow you to find, remember, and re-focus on your values, priorities and goals.

LAW OF ABUNDANCE
- Infinite resources
- Karma and Mazal

Most people think that resources as SCARCE ... some of the most frequent statements you will hear people and many times yourselves say are ... I don't have the time, I don't have the money, I don't have the energy ...

This is a consequence on focusing on a life based on "The Law of Scarcity". A world where there is not enough for everyone.

However, in reality, **resources are abundant! And infinite!!** There is enough of everything for everyone in this world.

And allow me to put a thought in your mind ... if you do not have something, it is usually because you have something else in your life instead. And following up from the previous rule I mentioned – attraction and focus – you are what you focus on, and you attract what you focus on.

I have used this law to change my approach to time, money and relationships amongst other parts of my life.

You see, until not long ago, **I actually believed I was poor**. No matter how much money I had, I always thought I was

71

poor. I would focus on life being a struggle, that I could not afford anything and that I would never be able to afford what I really wanted.

And I would not only think this, but I would tell people. I would complain about money, as a victim of my circumstances. I would even use the word "broke" in my conversations more times than you can think of.

Then I came to understand that being broke and being poor were not the same. Being poor is indeed a state of mind. If you think you are poor, no matter how much you have, you will always feel poor. On the other hand, being broke is just a condition, a temporary situation that you can fix by taking action.

Remember I am originally from Argentina, a Latino at heart and in personality – in many more ways that I would have liked some times – and thanks to this I recently came to meet a new group of people from South America. People that like me came with almost nothing to the UK …

Thanks to this I learnt how much of a better life you could have with much 'less'. Again, everything is relative, depending on how you want to see and live your life.

The experience made me realise, and also complemented with my studies, that everything is right and everything is always resolved, and it finds its way to a solution.

The other very clever and relevant part about abundance is that helps you be a giver, as you have infinite resources and everything you want and need. The interesting point about this is that the more you give, the more you receive, and the more it comes back to you. It may not be from the same place, but it will come back to you with interest. A note on this is that you need to remember that the opposite will occur if you act based on the law of scarcity. This is what many refer to as Karma, or as my new friend Laurence told me over dinner one night, Mazal!

6.2 EXTRAS – CONCEPTS & COMMON LIMITING BELIEVES

The following concepts and examples of common limiting believes are some I have observed firstly in myself, but also in many people I come across. By reviewing this, they will support your change process, as you may be able to observe some of them on yourself and others.

To start, I would like you to take a minute to think about this:

PLAY ATTITUDE & HOLIDAY MINDSET
I would like to propose to you to think again about approaching your life with what I call a **"play attitude"**. Just try observing children, whom under normal circumstances live a life with no worries or major responsibilities. All they think of is "playing" games and enjoying each day moment by moment. Or you can try to remember when you were a child and, for example, how excited you would get the night before and the day you were going on holidays. **#Holidaymindset**

Now I challenge you to assume this attitude and mindset every day as you go to bed, wake up and go about doing your business during the day. Go have that coffee in the local Italian, take 15 mins, seat outside to watch people go by ... go visit a place you have never been too ... do whatever you would do during a holiday!

COMMON LIMITING BELIEVES
Here are some examples that if you have them, you will be able to understand and change, and they will not stop you ever again from doing what you want.

i) Fear – Instincts vs. Self-doubt: What usually freezes and prevent you from acting. Fear is what stops us right in our tracks, always a couple of seconds or days after we dare to dream and get excited.

Fear will normally stop you from taking action: fear of ridicule, fear of loneliness, fear what people would say and think of you.

Dr. John Demartini, for example, talks of six main fears we face: age, losing love, poverty, illness, criticism, and death.

Understanding your fears may be useful, but when you focus on what it is really important and use the laws of the universe, you only need to focus on the opposite to your fears, focus on what you really want.

Having said this, I think it is important to differentiate between fear that comes from your instincts and the one that is pure self-doubt.

The fear that we feel as a consequence of our **instincts** is an automated self-survival reaction we experience when we are or presume to be in danger. Doctors and researchers insist that we should trust this instinct and apply the FFF rules – **Fight, Flight, and Freeze** – according to the situation.

On the other hand, self-doubt is just unfounded; there is usually no logic to it. The most important factor to refute any logic or rationale you come with to detract yourself from following through is ... that you are capable of anything your brain desires to do. In fact, if you recall **visualisations**, which we covered separately, you will remember that 1) your brain does not differentiate between what is real and not, and 2) what you visualise does in fact normally already exist in material form, or you just happened to have created in your mind and therefore made it possible in existence in a parallel world – as inventors do with any inventions.

An appendix to add to the self-doubt fear is **"irrational fear"**, which is when the animal side in our brain simply takes over and create **catastrophic situation** – a type of worst case scenario – in order to keep us from being hurt or feeling pain. This is mostly based upon past experiences or images and situations we have seen in the outside world. Please be very aware of this appendix fear thoughts, as for many of us it is the cause of making some of our worst decisions, taking drastic erratic actions and hurting people we love and ourselves in the process.

Key tip and action:
1) Try to differentiate the different type of fears you are experiencing between instinct or self-doubt basis.
2) Decide on FFF or work on your visualisations and reality to be able to calm you down and come down to reality.
3) Become mindful and aware. Focus on your actions to create a positive consequence based on your strengths.

ii) Prejudice: Goes hand in hand with the generation of fears and doubts, but not only of yourself but others. And because of the law of attraction, you will receive exactly what you feel and think of others as it all comes back to you.

Prejudice is a preconceived or created judgment or opinion, usually negative, without understanding of facts or all information on a matter, person or group or examination of the facts. It would materialise in the way of irrational suspicion or hatred of a particular group, race, or religion.

Action: just accept people for what they are; do not expect things to be only the way you think they are supposed to be. **Give love to others!** Give love to everyone! And it will come back to you with interest! Remember, we all try our best, within our qualities and limitations.

iii) Attachment & self worth: In the new world, starting with the western side, we find that people get attached to external things, be it material or what this "something" represents. The materiality could relate to wealth, accumulating money, or just things – houses, cars, clothes, watches, food, going out, travelling – as well as people – family, parents, partners, children, friends. At the same time, we all have our own hierarchies of where all these material things sit in our self imposed "scale", in relation to the various qualifications and added significance we add to them and what this material external objects project to people about us.

You see, the fallacy with this approach is that our value or and self-worth is linked to these attachments, and therefore are external to us, and in many ways than one – particularly when related to people – we cannot control. This is a very special prerogative we actually give away. We can actually go within ourselves and learn about ourselves, about our intrinsic value and learn to appreciate and value ourselves for who we are and how we act as a person, which will imminently bring all and more you can have in external "objects".

There is no better example to use on this case than Warren Buffet: watching a BBC documentary about him a while ago, I came across the richest man in the world, a man that has lived in the same house for the last 20+ years and does not have more material things at hand – car, offices, etc. – than any standard middle class person in the USA. I even found out for the first time, that although he was married to his wife, she actually left the marital home after 20 years of marriage to move to San Francisco, but the twist to the story is that they never divorced and he actually started

76

living with one of her friends 5 years after she moved and then married her only after his wife died.

I do not endorse anything this gentleman did or does, but what did strike me was that here was a person that set himself to accumulate so much wealth, while just trying to live by his values and within his own means and worth. I also wanted to mention that on his death he is not planning on living any inheritance to his children and is donating a large portion of his wealth to the Bill Gates Foundation. I just thought that he is actually a role model in so many ways, but I'll let you draw your own conclusions.

iv) **Stones we carry in life:** if I try to summarise this point, and as follow up to the point about "attachment", the "stones we carry with us" are those memories and people that we choose to keep in our lives, because of the fear of losing or not being able to find and feel the same again. Well, you will never find the same again, that's the beauty of uniqueness. But you may find something as special in its own right.

ACTIONS
Taking action is the one activity that makes all the difference in our lives, starting with your thoughts and managing your mind set, following with the activities and actual action taken to consistently make a difference in your life.

Action on its own has more impact when organised in the form of a plan, with specific and detailed tasks organised in the timeline, with dependencies and relations attached to one another.

Action: if you are able to first accept your situation, understand what it is you want to change, work out what is it you need to do, organise it, and take Action! Nothing can stop you from success, as you are succeeding already!

HELMS, STORMS, and ANCHORS
I want to use the analogy of sailing boats and anchors to explain the concept of "letting go" and "stabilising" your current situation.

A couple of years ago I went and took a sailing course and did some yacht racing around the Solent, in England. While I was taking the course, during the practical part at sea, I had the realisation of some analogies between some situations during the class and our everyday life.

The one lesson I remember thinking that was key to understanding problems or complicated situations was while we were practicing letting the helm go, the yacht starts turning around in order face the wind and nothing happens.

Apparently this is particularly helpful while facing a STORM, as nothing will happen and the yacht is very unlikely to capsize, as long as you put the sail down and DO NOT try to control the boat.

So this got me thinking, when we are in a situation in life where we do not know what to do, specially a storm, all we need to do is LET GO OF THE HELM ... and wait until the storm passes.

I know this sounds rather simplistic and we cannot extend this example to every situation in life – especially one of emergency – but if you think about all other situations you have faced in life, even those you thought were such an important event, everything always worked out or worked "itself" out in the end.

And since we are on the maritime analogies, I thought it would be good to mention something I use a lot on a day to day basis, as this is what I call my ANCHORS. Like a ship, I use these to stabilise myself or look for images that remind me the reason why I am doing what I am doing, these are reminders I place around my house or even as my screensaver on my iPhone, which prompt me to keep focused. These could be, for example, the picture of my children or just the view from my house. I also use them on couple of "vision boards" I have created.

Action: I highly recommend you do this daily and during the day, to keep remembering what is all about, and as a "help" to bring all those feeling from the subconscious mind to set you in the direction you want.

FAMILY, FRIENDS, SUPPORTING NETWORK AND GROUPS

There is yet another key part of life which many people, especially those that struggle with their feelings, tend to forget, push aside, or consciously disregard all together. This is the **need to share, discuss, philosophise and connect with others. The NEED for Family, Friends, Groups, Gangs, Committees, Glares, whatever you think is the type of people and groups you think you need to relate to in relation to your values, what you want to do, who you want to be and become.**

The one thing I have come to remember and realise is the importance of working out if the people we are relating to are really in line with whom we are and, most importantly, the person we want to be. If we decide that a friend or even a family member is not constructive to us, we can make an effort to manage the relationship in order to understand the challenges they are posing for us and find ways to focus on those that are more supportive towards our end goals.

These people act indeed as a support network. They help us bring out our best, as they give us the instance in which we can share what we think, feel, achieve, and so on.

More recently I have realised how many friends I currently have and I have leaned on them through my toughest periods. During this process I also made new friends, as I understood their importance and opened up to new people and share my life situation. Depending on the stage I was at, I found that people would kindly listen and identified with me at times, which is what gave me the chance to reciprocate. What followed were two (or more) people sharing life stories, experiences and current thoughts, resonating with each other and growing as individuals and as friends and relationships.

Some very specific points I realised I need to follow in order to make the most of the opportunity, which I didn't use to in the past, are:

Layers: people, just like you, have what I call "layers" – just like the onion – and it is for you to use your awareness to work out which layers you can share. You do not need to like or connect with every person at every level. So listen, talk, assess, and understand.

Invest time: in order to develop any relationship, you need to invest time. Just like with flowers and plants, you need to water your relationships, and give them space to absorb and grow at its own pace as well.

Accept: it is paramount you accept people for who they are, how they think and behave. I try to learn from what I can learn from people and accept the differences. The moment we start judging people, we are in fact using our values to assess their behaviour and this usually causes only two things – Your disappointment and their rejection.

Cycles and stages: as we grow and change with time and experiences, we tend to need new people in our lives, to continue through cycles and stages in life. At the same time, the people we already know keep evolving and changing, going through their own cycles. What is important to understand, learn and do as we go through this process, is to be able to spend the right amount of time with the people who are in line with us, our values and our goals. Rather than being upset for spending less time with somebody, or even let go of the person all together, let us try to understand why this is happening, and remember that everything happens for a good reason. Live, learn and accept!

6.3 THE CREATIVE PROCESS

Now, taking into consideration all that has been mentioned until now, I would like to synthesise for you the amazing "Creative Process".

I also learnt this concept thanks to 'The Secret', and it is one I use as much as possible to make things happen for me.

I have indeed tried to simplify the process for my own benefit.

Think about it like this: **"You can only have what you think and believe you deserve".**

Or think about it the other way around: "You CANNOT receive anything in life that you think you DO NOT deserve"

The creative process is summarised with the three steps: **Ask … Believe … Receive! #ABR**

You ask for what you want, you believe as if you already have it, and the opportunity comes to you, and you have to receive it.

During the process, and most importantly when the time to receive, it is only with "Awareness" that we are able to "embrace" and complete the creation process.

Awareness is the most important component that brings together the **trident!** To me, the moment in which we see the creative process *materialising in front of our own eyes*, is the moment when you need to **embrace** what you asked for.

GOALS, PLANS AND STRATEGIES

"Set a goal to achieve something that is so BIG, so exhilarating that it excites you and scares you at the same time. It must be a goal that is so appealing, so much in line with your spiritual core (vision and dream), that you can't get it out of your mind ..."

Bob Proctor

Now you know who you want to be, what you want in life, as a person, emotionally or sentimentally, materially, you need to structure your actions in a way that you can follow each step until you achieved what you have set yourself to do.

How do you do this? Simple! ... You set out what is exactly that you want to achieve, you set plans (or projects and streams) – one to start is ok– and strategies to encompass our plans on how you will run these plans to achieve your goals.

If one fails or does not work. Then you re-write it and try again.

PVSPPA – PURPOSE, VISION, STRATEGY, PLAN, PASSION, ACTION

This is a system I use to make my own dreams come true. From a creative process of wishing, imagining, feeling what you want, I believe we need a structure and more specific knowledge and actions to achieve them.

More specifically, this system is called **PVSPPA**. And I summarise the key components for you below.

PURPOSE: this is the reason **WHY** you do what you do. It is the reason why you exist in this life, and is at your core, representing all you are. To find this you need to find yourself first, and doing the priorities and values exercise – in chapter 3 – will most definitely get you closer to understanding yourself a bit better.

VISION: this is the **HORIZON** to where you want to go, and where you want people to follow. It helps if it is big enough to excite you and others, yet possible to reach. But hey, we know anything is possible! So make sure you have it clear and can explain to others.

STRATEGY: this is the **APPROACH** you are going to go about achieving your vision and living your purpose. You can start at a high level and go down to the lowest detailed level.

PLAN: you will need to set a plan to break down all the activities you need to carry out to achieve your vision and living your purpose.

PASSION: you will need to be passionate from your **HEART** about what you are doing. But you know what? If you are following your purpose in life, the passion comes to you every day, every morning ... and it pulls you towards that dream !

ACTION: you need to take action, every day, every week. No matter what you do, just take action and you will get there ... ! **COMPOUNDING ... all the way !**

CHAPTER 7
HEALTH (& EXERCISE) AND PERSONAL FINANCES & FINANCIAL INTELIGENCE

I finish the book with these subjects, in order to highlight the importance they have to start, support and maintain your success.

While reading several books, attending seminars, and doing research to improve my own life and to write this book, I have come to realise that there are two fundamental points that are either covered in most books in a rather minimal way, or not at all: **Health and Finances**

7.1 HEALTH (& EXERCISE)
Let's start by highlighting what an incredible and sophisticated machine we have in the form of our body – which includes your powerful mind. Is the most amazing piece of equipment, is self-sufficient and even capable of self-healing.

The funniest or most challenging thing is that we are not taught to appreciate the complexity and magical gift we have been given at birth, and most of us take it as a given and for granted.

What is also amazing and for the same reason, many times we see people who do all sorts to their body through an unhealthy life style, yet the machine keeps working and plodding on like a "little donkey with a heavy load".

Health: Simple: No health ... no life! Put a sticker on your forehead ...☺ ... "LOOK AFTER YOURSELF"!

This is the one single factor in our lives that we can't do without. The importance of having good health is normally overlooked and underestimated by most of us, until the day we either lose it ourselves or see somebody close affected by it.

I am after all a qualified Personal Trainer and Nutritionist, and I had struggled to look after myself properly, mainly because the battle is usually against the **old habits**.

This is why it is key to understand what drives us in life and to have an "end-game" or strong enough "target" to be able to commit (motivate) to achieving, and most importantly, maintaining! Consistently!

If I had to attempt to summarise the various parts of a day and how to approach it in order to have a healthy life, I would go for;

One word: **"balanced"**.

Three areas: **Create (Work), Play, and Rest (Relax/Sleep)** or,

Nine main activities: **Eat, work (create), eat, exercise, eat, work, relax, eat, and sleep** ... and **REPEAT** *it all over again*

I insist to say that you already know what I am saying here, so all I am doing yet again is reminding you and perhaps highlighting or presenting some approaches that you may not know in a different way.

i) Sleep: I would like to start with the last step mentioned in the main activities of the day above, what I think to be the mother of all needs to have good health: **SLEEP!**

Until very recently, I never truly understood and appreciated the need and effects of sleeping. I would push myself to the limit constantly, fighting the bed time and allocating the minimum possible amount of hours to sleeping. I would go to be close to midnight and be up by 5-6 AM. Even on the weekend, I would push myself to fitting one more film at night to get up early in the morning to go to the gym or play golf … to make "the most of my day and my life" I would say. And to make things worse, I would see it as a waste of time not to do it.

In all honesty, the obsession was affected by the years when I used to work in Banking-Mergers & Acquisitions where, some days during busy weeks, I would work from 8-9am until 3-4AM the next day, or 24 hours straight in the office with no sleep at all. When I moved from this role to a new one, I said to myself:

"If you can do that for others - a job and a company, why can't you do the same for yourself."

What I failed to see was the effect that not resting or sleeping enough had on me, my brain, the way I acted during the day and the consequences of my decisions and on the people that loved me.

Also, as you get older, the "recovery" time is longer, and therefore – as when you are growing as a baby – the more you do, the more rest you need.
Main Objective: try to sleep 8 Hours a day! Do whatever it takes to achieve this.

ii) Eat: eating is another area that gets overlooked, to the point that we actually are willing to give up meals in order to produce more work or simply save money.

The super machine we have needs energy to function and this energy is created mainly if we eat. And we achieve a better performance if the energy is constant.

So I will use the one word mentioned previously to summarise how you need to think of your diet: **balanced!**

Think about it this way, the super machine needs various ingredients inside to make the most of you. I will try to make it very simple for you, so just try to think of water, vitamins, healthy fats, carbohydrates, proteins whenever you are doing your daily or weekly shopping. You can find books or Google lists that give you examples, but in simplified terms you need to think of a piece of meat – preferable fish and chicken, some brown rice or sweet potatoes, salads, fruits , vegetables, and 3-5 litres of water a day.

Tip: to keep your energy levels steady is to eat several smaller portions of food every 2-3 hours. The key for success here, like in everything in life, involves at least a little bit of planning.

Main Objective: eat at least 5 balanced meals a day.

iii) Meditate: meditating is so much more than what we realise. There are many ways to meditate; you just need to find the type that works for you.

I recommend you to also do your own little bit of research if you would like to find out more about it. You can start by reading the Wikipedia link below:
http://en.wikipedia.org/wiki/Meditation

I personally have always found it difficult to meditate on my own, so I had joined groups, which also helped me to expand my horizons. As my life evolved however, where I moved countries and cities I was not able to keep the same groups.

Finally I was introduced to *Mindfulness*, which has helped me significantly, as I basically can use it at anytime, anywhere. In brief, what mindfulness allows you not do is to get out of your own thoughts and concentrate on the now through something you can focus on.

For example: a couple of mindfulness activators I used are my mobile phone, as well as the trees by the motorway, or simply my breathing and organs as I am talking to people.

I still recommend you take even 5 minutes at the beginning and end of the day. Do this even if it is as part of your gratitude and visualizations routines. This time will be in fact the key moment for your creative process, and will help you immensely. It will help you to conquer all your dreams!

iv) Exercise: think about exercising as a way to keeping and even making yourself younger! And this is in fact true!

If this is not enough good reasons, think about whatever you need to visualise to commit to doing it 3 to 6 times a week.

It is simply about making it another habit in your life, part of your life ... your life!

Exercising keeps the machine forcing to regenerate itself from a physical perspective. From a mental perspective, it is proven that also releases several chemicals that help you feel better.

Exercise can take all sorts of forms; you can do it at home (push ups, abs, DVDs), on the street (walk, run, bike), or join a gym (cardio, weights, classes).

Tip: if you can, try to find a training buddy.

Main Objective: exercise once a day, between 3 to 6 times a week.

Note: exercise is one of the 3 most important things you should do every day, hopefully before 11AM to get the best result (and out of the way early in the day ;-), straight after meditating and visualising. This is fact what many of the most successful people in the world do.

I highly recommend using YouTube to get ideas of what you can do. There is a world of ideas on that site; you just need to find what works for you.

Just to give you a real example, I once became one of the best tennis players I could be in my club, using YouTube to learn techniques

v) Work: I like to think about work with a "Play attitude" too. This has helped me a lot in terms of approaching it in a more relaxed way, and when applying all the other skills and habits mentioned in this book, it helps substantially when dealing with others.

I now also think about work as "creating", using my mind to generate ideas and projects, and challenging myself in order to achieve the best I can, whilst working and helping others to push our limits.

If you take into consideration the lessons and tips mentioned throughout the book, you will be able to find your vocation and end up doing what you really love for a living, and the level of energy and ideas you will generate will be unbelievable.

For those that need to work with what they currently have, while creating a plan to become who they want to be, this approach will help you **love and enjoy** your current job and achieve much more than you ever thought was possible, whilst enjoying your life significantly more too.

vi) Relax: this word gets usually confused, and we actually think we are "relaxing", when we are actually "procrastinating".

Relaxing is important to give our brains and bodies a break from all the thinking and physical activities we take on. It can take the shape of a conversation or dinner with friends, a tennis match, reading a book.

This step in your daily activities gives you a break in order to help you expand your horizons or simply "disconnect" from everything else, or connect to another level.

Simple tool: Daily timeline/timetable focus: The Picture below is an example of one of my initial daily timelines I created to help me focus through my day. In it you may find some of the concepts I had learnt and applied in order to change my life.

I recommend you create your own, just as a guide or direction or a compass to go back to when you need to remember ...

You can use a timetable, or excel, or even hand write it:

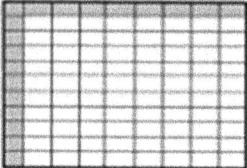

Or you can make it as simple as the below example of a hand written version:

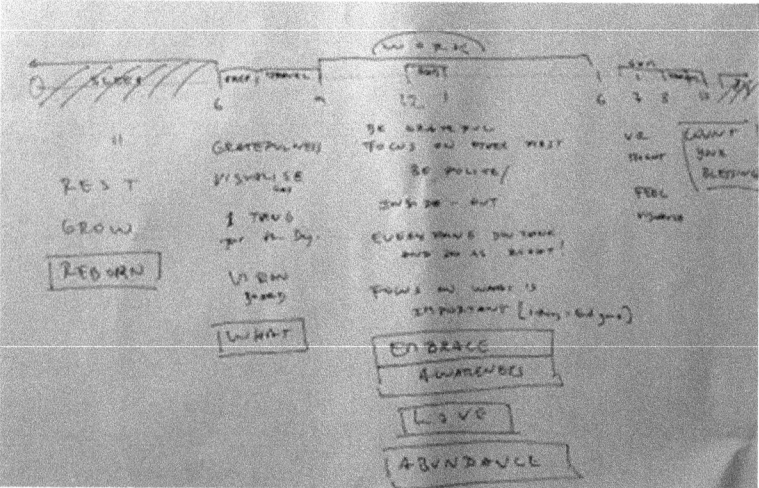

7.2 PERSONAL FINANCES & FINANCIAL INTELIGENCE

The one final concept that you would think "should" be the easiest for me, somehow feels like the most difficult to cover, given my education, qualifications and experience. Yet these are also the most essential "lessons or perspective" that I was never taught by my parents, or at school and university.

I want to finish the book with one practical concept, which is important to master in order to manage your finances in the most effective way. I want to talk about the most basic concepts of personal finances.

Why is it important to learn this concept? Because once you internalise the various lessons I have shared in this book, and thanks to your new understanding on how to become happy and successful, you will be able to enjoy your life even more ... if you manage your finances correctly.

I have a degree in management and economics, and a master in international finance, but I had never been taught and explained the most basic concept and "perspective" of personal finances. For the same reason, as well as struggling with emotional intelligence, many people struggle with financial intelligence. I cannot argue that both are related in many ways, but you can still manage to master one without the other in certain ways too. However, if you are not even aware of them, it is virtually impossible.

The same way I think that the various concepts touched upon in this book will help improve your "emotional intelligence", the following paragraphs will give you a quick insight in potentially improving your "financial intelligence" too.

As with the other parts of the book, I want to make this as simple and summarised as possible, and for that I would like to touch upon the following points:

Assets vs. Liabilities: The first difference I want to share and highlight is the one I think could help improve your financial intelligence, and your financial situation going forwards, as well as that of your close ones forever.

Asset and liabilities are terms at the core of any accountancy course, and it would in simple terms relate to what you own vs. what you owe respectively, representing in a way the two sides of a coin.

After many years of study and working in an industry that focuses on these same terms, I came across a book that presented the terms in a way which I never heard before. A practical approach to it, which I think would help many people grasp in order to improve the way they look at money and as a consequence their personal finances.

The book is called "Rich Dad ... Poor Dad" by Robert Kiyosaki. As with my other recommendations, I urge you to read this book, when you are ready and want to make the time for it.

I do not attempt to repeat or summarise what is written is Robert's book, but I would like to explain in my words what I understood and found useful, in case you find it useful or resonates with you.

I am going to start with **Liabilities**, which is any **outgoing from your pocket** that is in simple terms **an expense**, and it does not generate any income or revenues for you. Going out, eating out, food, and more shockingly, buying a car or even a house are all "liabilities".

A house you may ask? Yes! A house! Because unless you are renting the house out and generating a profit – a positive differential between what you pay in mortgage/maintenance and the rent paid to you – you are actually spending money, out of your cash.

On the opposite side - and you can use the example of the house again - an **Asset** is an outgoing you have that generates **income or revenue** for you, and potentially profits if managed properly.

What you want to aim to achieve with your finances is to "spend" your money/cash in "Assets".

This brings us to the next term I want to highlight:
Cash flow: Most people find it hard to navigate through life in order to meet their commitment and spend most days "working to pay the bills".

You will find, that most people think if "they had more money" they would be happier, or they would have a better life. But the truth is that unless you know how to manage your money, and unless you understand your values and drivers, you will find that these same people struggle to be happy and keep spending more than they earn. This is what in simple financial terms means a "cash flow" problem, where the money/cash that goes out of your account is higher that the amount/cash that goes in.

Spending more than you earn is one of the most common problems people face. This can be for various reasons, some associated to unforeseen events (like an accident), poor planning (like not budgeting for known events), or simply being driven by short term satisfaction (like shopping things what we do not need).

Even wealthy people sometimes face cash flow problems, although they would always have the option of selling some of their assets (or liabilities) – depending on liquidity – to generate more cash.

Wealth: Wealth is the abundance of valuable resources or material possessions. Please note the word "Abundance"! But from what I explained above, if you think of resources and materials possessions from an Asset vs. Liabilities perspective, which possessions will make you wealthier? Correct: assets!

Liquidity: This is the term we use to express how quickly you can sell or convert your possessions into cash. The more liquid, the quicker you can sell. For example, stocks and shares in large public companies as usually seen as one of the most liquid possessions (assets) we can have, or simpler things like gold.

Your house for example, takes longer to sell and therefore is less liquid or illiquid.

Portfolio: The term use to refer to the group of investments we have. In general, the recommendation is to have a "diversified" portfolio, in order to manage/spread/diversify your risk. However, from what we learn in this book and from examples such us that given by the likes of billionaire Warren Buffet, the key is to understand the risk and what you are investing in.

Investing in what you love: One very important point we made earlier in the book is the power of love, and the immense benefits you can draw from doing what you really love. The same applies to investing: if you invest in something you love, you are several times more likely to want to learn and understand the investment and consequently understand the risk and therefore increase your chances of success.

Risk: Here is a concept you will find in all the finance books and that has actually been terrifying the city during the past yeas.

In simple terms, everything has a risk. Different types of risks. So the key is to understand what they are and how you can manage them.

Savings: I do not want to disregard savings; it is a very good and noble thing to do. We should teach others and learn to do it, but I believe that it should be with a view that considers all the terms and concepts mentioned in this section.

There is one thing and one thing only you need to focus on … and that is … CREATE ASSETS & LIVE BELOW YOUR MEANS! … But you will only be able to do so if you manage your feelings, your subconscious mind, your HABITS!

THE END

Have the most Amazing, Wonderful, Happy and Successful life!!!

FINAL RECAP

I hope you enjoyed this book and you have found it useful. In order to remember the formula you may want to find the best model that suits you. In my case, my brain likes images, and this is why I use the set of blocks and pillars I showed you at the beginning of the book.

At this point you may also find it easier to understand how you want to structure and manage yourself, in order to maintain the changes you have achieved in the years to come.

As I said before, I do not expect you to agree with everything I put forward in this book, but if you take at least one thing that helps you be happier - Let alone more successful or achieve one of your many dreams - you are helping us both achieve part of this amazing goal! Thank you!

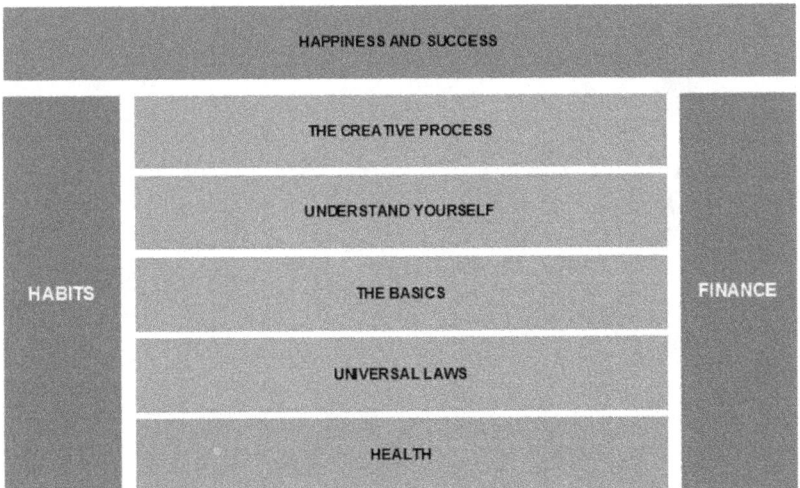

	HAPPINESS AND SUCCESS	
	THE CREATIVE PROCESS	
	UNDERSTAND YOURSELF	
HABITS	THE BASICS	FINANCE
	UNIVERSAL LAWS	
	HEALTH	

Remember ... *"LIFE IS A MARATHON ... NOT A RACE"*
So ... start "COMPOUNDING" ... right NOW!

OTHER ACKNOWLEDGEMENTS

I also want to thank some specific people who inspired me and shared their knowledge in the past, as I am doing with you today:

Rhonda Byrne
Napoleon Hill
Bob Proctor
John Assaraf
Dr. John Demartini
Dale Carnegie
Deepak Chopra
Robert Kiyosaki
Anthony Robins
Warren Buffett
Stephen Covey
Louise hay
Will Smith
Tyrese Gibson
Dr. Wayne W. Dyer

About JP TI

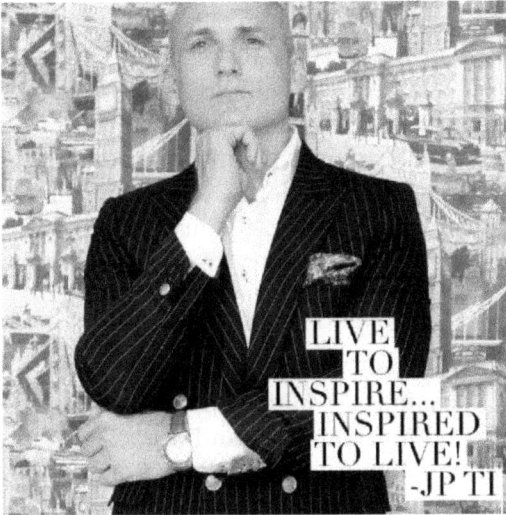

LIVE TO INSPIRE... INSPIRED TO LIVE!
-JP TI

JP's purpose and passion in life is in furthering the lives of others. He is a Transformational Inspirer, International Banking professional, Advisor, Public Speaker, Mentor, Author and Writer. He is committed to enhancing the future of society by helping and inspiring people to transform their lives and achieve their full potential, as well as advising businesses to find, create and manage the required changes that will bring them the results they want, and take them to the top of their chosen industry.

Throughout his professional career JP has had exposure to and successfully helped manage the performance and change of multi-billion, cross-regional, 30+ countries footprint businesses, including specific stakeholder and sponsor roles for multi-million programmes and their business coordination and management, from idea inception to development and delivery.

He has been a key team member at CEO and Executive office level at some of the largest Banks and Professional Services companies in the world, consistently achieving his personal and professional goals while holding various roles during the past 15 years.

He also has experience with and exposure to start-ups and SMEs, having created, ran and advised several companies in various sectors in executive as well as non-executive roles, and he is an advisor to not-for-profit organizations, focusing on young leaders of the future, creating exceptional opportunities to inspire and empower young people to develop a mind-set for success, helping them learn best practices to fulfill their aspirations.

JP is the proud father of two daughters. He holds a M.Sc. in Business Management, Economics and Accountancy with distinction, and a Post-graduate degree in International Finance. He speaks fluent Spanish.

NOTES

www.ingramcontent.com/pod-product-compliance
Lightning Source LLC
Chambersburg PA
CBHW051431090426
42737CB00014B/2923